Student Planner

for Learning and Growing!

Homeschool Edition

Activinotes

Activinotes

DAILY JOURNALS, PLANNERS, NOTEBOOKS AND OTHER BLANK BOOKS

Student Planner

Notes:

_____
_____
_____
_____
_____
_____
_____
_____
_____
_____
_____
_____
_____
_____
_____
_____
_____
_____
_____
_____

Reminders   Jots

Student Planner

To do list

Notes

Day / Time	Subject	Activities	Description

Student Planner

Notes :

_____
_____
_____
_____
_____
_____
_____
_____
_____
_____
_____
_____
_____
_____
_____
_____
_____
_____
_____
_____
_____

Assignments   Tests & Exams

Student Planner

To do list

Notes

Day / Time	Subject	Activities	Description

Student Planner

Notes:

_____
_____
_____
_____
_____
_____
_____
_____
_____
_____
_____
_____
_____
_____
_____
_____
_____
_____
_____

Assignments	Tests & Exams

Student Planner

To do list

Notes

Day / Time	Subject	Activities	Description

Student Planner

Notes :

Assignments   Tests & Exams

Student Planner

To do list

Notes

Day / Time	Subject	Activities	Description

Student Planner

Notes :

Assignments

Tests & Exams

Student Planner

To do list   Notes

Day / Time	Subject	Activities	Description

Student Planner

Notes :

Assignments   Tests & Exams

Student Planner

To do list	Notes

Day / Time	Subject	Activities	Description

Student Planner

Notes :

_____

_____

_____

_____

_____

_____

_____

_____

_____

_____

_____

_____

_____

_____

_____

_____

_____

_____

_____

_____

Assignments   Tests & Exams

Student Planner

To do list   Notes

Day / Time	Subject	Activities	Description

Student Planner

Notes :

_____
_____
_____
_____
_____
_____
_____
_____
_____
_____
_____
_____
_____
_____
_____
_____
_____
_____
_____
_____

Assignments   Tests & Exams

Student Planner

Name: Age: School Level:

To do list   Notes

Day / Time	Subject	Activities	Description

Student Planner

Notes :

Assignments

Tests & Exams

Student Planner

To do list

Notes

Day / Time	Subject	Activities	Description

Student Planner

Notes :

Assignments

Tests & Exams

Student Planner

To do list

Notes

Day / Time	Subject	Activities	Description

Student Planner

Notes :

_____
_____
_____
_____
_____
_____
_____
_____
_____
_____
_____
_____
_____
_____
_____
_____
_____
_____
_____
_____
_____

Assignments   Tests & Exams

Student Planner

Name: Age: School Level:

To do list

Notes

Day / Time	Subject	Activities	Description

Student Planner

Notes :

_____
_____
_____
_____
_____
_____
_____
_____
_____
_____
_____
_____
_____
_____
_____
_____
_____
_____
_____
_____

Assignments   Tests & Exams

Student Planner

	To do list	Notes

Day / Time	Subject	Activities	Description

Student Planner

Notes :

_____
_____
_____
_____
_____
_____
_____
_____
_____
_____
_____
_____
_____
_____
_____
_____
_____
_____
_____
_____

Assignments   Tests & Exams

Student Planner

To do list

Notes

Day / Time	Subject	Activities	Description

Student Planner

Notes :

_____
_____
_____
_____
_____
_____
_____
_____
_____
_____
_____
_____
_____
_____
_____
_____
_____
_____
_____
_____
_____
_____
_____

Assignments

Tests & Exams

Student Planner

To do list   Notes

Day / Time	Subject	Activities	Description

Student Planner

Notes :
_____
_____
_____
_____
_____
_____
_____
_____
_____
_____
_____
_____
_____
_____
_____
_____
_____
_____
_____
_____
_____
_____

Assignments   Tests & Exams

Student Planner

Name: Age: School Level:

To do list

Notes

Day / Time	Subject	Activities	Description

Student Planner

Notes :

Assignments   Tests & Exams

Student Planner

To do list

Notes

Day / Time	Subject	Activities	Description

Student Planner

Notes :

Assignments

Tests & Exams

Student Planner

To do list

Notes

Day / Time	Subject	Activities	Description

Student Planner

Notes :
_____
_____
_____
_____
_____
_____
_____
_____
_____
_____
_____
_____
_____
_____
_____
_____
_____
_____
_____

Assignments   Tests & Exams

Student Planner

To do list   Notes

Day / Time	Subject	Activities	Description

Student Planner

Notes :

Assignments · Tests & Exams

Student Planner

To do list

Notes

Day / Time	Subject	Activities	Description

Student Planner

Notes :

_____
_____
_____
_____
_____
_____
_____
_____
_____
_____
_____
_____
_____
_____
_____
_____
_____
_____
_____
_____
_____
_____

Assignments   Tests & Exams

Student Planner

Name: Age: School Level:

To do list

Notes

Day / Time	Subject	Activities	Description

Student Planner

Notes :

_____
_____
_____
_____
_____
_____
_____
_____
_____
_____
_____
_____
_____
_____
_____
_____
_____
_____
_____
_____
_____
_____
_____

Assignments   Tests & Exams

Student Planner

To do list

Notes

Day / Time	Subject	Activities	Description

Student Planner

Notes:

_____
_____
_____
_____
_____
_____
_____
_____
_____
_____
_____
_____
_____
_____
_____
_____
_____
_____
_____
_____
_____
_____
_____

Assignments   Tests & Exams

Student Planner

To do list   Notes

Day / Time	Subject	Activities	Description

Student Planner

Notes :

Assignments

Tests & Exams

Student Planner

To do list

Notes

Day / Time	Subject	Activities	Description

Student Planner

Notes:

_____
_____
_____
_____
_____
_____
_____
_____
_____
_____
_____
_____
_____
_____
_____
_____
_____
_____
_____
_____

Assignments   Tests & Exams

Student Planner

To do list

Notes

Day / Time	Subject	Activities	Description

Student Planner

Notes :

_____
_____
_____
_____
_____
_____
_____
_____
_____
_____
_____
_____
_____
_____
_____
_____
_____
_____
_____
_____

Assignments   Tests & Exams

Student Planner

To do list	Notes

Day / Time	Subject	Activities	Description

Student Planner

Notes :

Assignments

Tests & Exams

Student Planner

To do list

Notes

Day / Time	Subject	Activities	Description

Student Planner

Notes :

Assignments   Tests & Exams

Student Planner

To do list   Notes

Day / Time	Subject	Activities	Description

Student Planner

Notes :

_____
_____
_____
_____
_____
_____
_____
_____
_____
_____
_____
_____
_____
_____
_____
_____
_____
_____

Assignments   Tests & Exams

Student Planner

Name: Age: School Level:

To do list

Notes

☐
☐
☐
☐
☐
☐
☐
☐
☐
☐

Day / Time	Subject	Activities	Description

Student Planner

Notes :

_____
_____
_____
_____
_____
_____
_____
_____
_____
_____
_____
_____
_____
_____
_____
_____
_____
_____

Assignments

Tests & Exams

Student Planner

Name: Age: School Level:

To do list

Notes

Day / Time	Subject	Activities	Description

Student Planner

Notes :

_____
_____
_____
_____
_____
_____
_____
_____
_____
_____
_____
_____
_____
_____
_____
_____
_____
_____
_____
_____
_____
_____

Assignments   Tests & Exams

Student Planner

To do list   Notes

Day / Time	Subject	Activities	Description

Student Planner

Notes :

_____
_____
_____
_____
_____
_____
_____
_____
_____
_____
_____
_____
_____
_____
_____
_____
_____
_____
_____
_____
_____
_____
_____
_____

Assignments   Tests & Exams

Student Planner

To do list	Notes

Day / Time	Subject	Activities	Description

Student Planner

Notes:

Assignments

Tests & Exams

Student Planner

To do list

Notes

Day / Time	Subject	Activities	Description

Student Planner

Notes :

Assignments

Tests & Exams

Student Planner

To do list

Notes

Day / Time	Subject	Activities	Description

Student Planner

Notes :

_____
_____
_____
_____
_____
_____
_____
_____
_____
_____
_____
_____
_____
_____
_____
_____
_____
_____
_____
_____
_____

Assignments

Tests & Exams

Student Planner

To do list   Notes

Day / Time	Subject	Activities	Description

Student Planner

Notes :

_____
_____
_____
_____
_____
_____
_____
_____
_____
_____
_____
_____
_____
_____
_____
_____
_____
_____
_____
_____

Assignments

Tests & Exams

Student Planner

To do list	Notes

Day / Time	Subject	Activities	Description

Student Planner

Notes :

_____
_____
_____
_____
_____
_____
_____
_____
_____
_____
_____
_____
_____
_____
_____
_____
_____
_____
_____
_____
_____
_____
_____

Assignments   Tests & Exams

Student Planner

To do list   ## Notes

Day / Time	Subject	Activities	Description

Student Planner

Notes :

Assignments

Tests & Exams

Student Planner

To do list

Notes

Day / Time	Subject	Activities	Description

Student Planner

Notes :

Assignments

Tests & Exams

Student Planner

To do list

Notes

Day / Time	Subject	Activities	Description

Student Planner

Notes:

Assignments

Tests & Exams

Student Planner

Name: Age: School Level:

To do list

Notes

Day / Time	Subject	Activities	Description

Student Planner

Notes :

Assignments   Tests & Exams

Student Planner

To do list

Notes

Day / Time	Subject	Activities	Description

Student Planner

Notes :

Assignments   Tests & Exams

Student Planner

To do list

Notes

Day / Time	Subject	Activities	Description

Student Planner

Notes :

_____
_____
_____
_____
_____
_____
_____
_____
_____
_____
_____
_____
_____
_____
_____
_____
_____
_____
_____
_____
_____

Assignments   Tests & Exams

Student Planner

To do list   Notes

Day / Time	Subject	Activities	Description

Student Planner

Notes :

_____
_____
_____
_____
_____
_____
_____
_____
_____
_____
_____
_____
_____
_____
_____
_____
_____
_____
_____
_____
_____
_____
_____
_____

Assignments   Tests & Exams

Student Planner

Name: Age: School Level:

To do list

Notes

Day / Time	Subject	Activities	Description

Student Planner

Notes:

_____
_____
_____
_____
_____
_____
_____
_____
_____
_____
_____
_____
_____
_____
_____
_____
_____
_____
_____
_____
_____

Assignments   Tests & Exams

Student Planner

To do list   Notes

Day / Time	Subject	Activities	Description

Student Planner

Notes :

Assignments

Tests & Exams

Student Planner

Name: Age: School Level:

To do list   Notes

☐
☐
☐
☐
☐
☐
☐
☐
☐

Day / Time	Subject	Activities	Description

Student Planner

Notes :

_____
_____
_____
_____
_____
_____
_____
_____
_____
_____
_____
_____
_____
_____
_____
_____
_____
_____
_____
_____
_____
_____

Assignments   Tests & Exams

Student Planner

To do list   Notes

Day / Time	Subject	Activities	Description

Student Planner

Notes :

Assignments

Tests & Exams

Student Planner

To do list   Notes

Day / Time	Subject	Activities	Description

Student Planner

Notes :

Assignments

Tests & Exams

Student Planner

To do list

☐
☐
☐
☐
☐
☐
☐
☐
☐

Notes

Day / Time	Subject	Activities	Description

Student Planner

Notes :

Assignments

Tests & Exams

Student Planner

To do list

Notes

Day / Time	Subject	Activities	Description

Student Planner

Notes :

_____

_____

_____

_____

_____

_____

_____

_____

_____

_____

_____

_____

_____

_____

_____

_____

_____

_____

_____

_____

Assignments   Tests & Exams

Student Planner

Name: Age: School Level:

To do list

Notes

Day / Time	Subject	Activities	Description

Student Planner

Notes :

Assignments   Tests & Exams

Student Planner

Name: Age: School Level:

To do list

Notes

Day / Time	Subject	Activities	Description

Student Planner

Notes :

Assignments   Tests & Exams

www.ingramcontent.com/pod-product-compliance
Lightning Source LLC
Chambersburg PA
CBHW081336090426
42737CB00017B/3175